Bigfoot and Woolybooger Tales

By Judith Victoria Hensley

Bigfoot and Woolybooger Tales

Judith Victoria Hensley

ISBN-13:
978-1986880053

ISBN-10:
1986880052

Printed by Create Space, an Amazon.com Company
CreateSpace, Charleston, SC

www.CreateSpace.com/TITLEID

Available from Amazon.com, CreateSpace.com, and other retail outlets

Cover Design: Judith Victoria Hensley

Cover Image: Public Domain Free Clipart Library

Dedication

To readers old and young who love a good tale and have an imagination big enough to believe

Thank You

To storytellers who still love to gather on the back porch, in front of the fireplace, or around a campfire and share the stories handed down from other generations or experienced personally.

To those who value seeing a story in print and the joy of holding a book in their hands.

To Jennifer McDaniels who made introductions and connections for me to the bigfoot researchers interviewed for this book

To Daniel Benoit, Jimmy Blanton, and Ed Brown who invited me to do a live interview with them on their shows

To Brian Ingermann for sharing his artwork

From the Author

I am a story gatherer. The intent of this book is not to prove or disprove the existence of bigfoot. The sole purpose is to gather stories from story tellers for the simple pleasure of the story.

I have never seen bigfoot, but if he's anywhere that I happen to be in the woods, I would love to have a camera in hand and see him/her for myself. The fact that I have not personally seen one does not cause me to doubt the sincerity of the stories in this book.

When I typed in "bigfoot" in a search engine, the number of sites listed was a staggering 30,500,000. Stories of this elusive cryptid are told around the globe. Sightings are continually being reported and many more exist that have never been recorded. Obviously, something is out there that people see and describe as bigfoot.

Read and decide for yourself.

Table of Contents

If you have had an encounter of your own or a good story from a reliable source that you'd like to share for a future publication, please follow instructions at the back of this book on pages 143-144

Public Domain Image

Some Other Names of Bigfoot
(Heard by the author in the region over the years.)

Sasquatch

Yeti

Yowie

Yaehoo

Ape Man

Yape Man

Wild Man

Hairy Man

Forest Man

Old Ones

Bush Man

Wild Man of the Woods

Skunk Ape

Windigo

Orang Pendek

Abominable Snowman

Elder Brother

Stone Man

Stone Giants

Woodland Spirit

Stink Beast

Big Man of the Woods

Giant of the Woods

Stinkapoo

Skunk Man

Guardians of the Forest

The Big Hairy Men

Woolybooger

Woodbooger

Booger Man

Forest Devil

Hairy Giants

Hairy People of the Woods

Man Monkey

Shug Monkey

Hillbilly Beast

Shag Nasty

Elusive Ones

The Watchers

Elder Brothers

The Earliest Recorded Bigfoot Encounter
By Judith Victoria Hensley

I have never seen a bigfoot, sasquatch, yeti, or ape man. I'm not sure I would want to unless it was a safe distance away from inside a car. However, the fact that I have not seen one does not mean that I would discredit those who say they have with great conviction.

Just as the eyewitness accounts of black panthers are very real to me because I've seen them myself, I acknowledge the many accounts of people who say they have seen bigfoot (by any name).

In both cases, black panther, and bigfoot, there are several reasons unrelated to myself or my own personal experience which convince me that others have seen what they say they have.

First of all, Native American culture from many different nations within North America have oral histories, art, drawings, and legends that have been handed down through generations about the large hairy manlike creatures that have come to be known as bigfoot.

I am persuaded that historically these cultures were simply recording information from the natural world around them. They did not create woolybooger stories to try and frighten themselves or those who would come generations after they passed. They could have cared less about a group of skeptics hundreds of years into the future who said that all the sightings were mistaken identities or hoaxes.

Daniel Boone recorded an encounter that he had with a very large hairy man, supposedly a ten-foot hairy giant. Written mentions of bigfoot go back to the first observations and writings of the European settlers as they fanned out across the new land.

To me, those are impressive accounts, because they were writing from their own experience, and in their time and place, without thought of future generations challenging the truth of what they were reporting.

From history lessons, I recall the earliest recorded bigfoot encounter has a date of 986 AD by Viking explorer Leif Ericson and his men as they explored North America.

Bayeux Tapestry 1077 public domain

Image from Mary MacGregor:
Stories of the Vikings 1908

I find it amusing that the big, burly, often ruthless Viking warrior explorers described these creatures as "horribly ugly, hairy, swarthy, and with great black eyes." They also noted a foul smell associated with the creature.

Coming from big burly, hairy, swarthy Vikings who probably did not bathe often in their exploits, it seems to me that these comments are like the pot calling the kettle black.

Whomever, or whatever they encountered, the experiences encouraged them to move on to other parts unknown for their explorations.

In Australia, according to Wikipedia, the first recorded account of the yowie (Australian bigfoot) was in 1795 and reports continue through modern times.

Johann Gehrts – 1887
Public Domain image

The Wild Man of Orford, England
Gathered from Wikipedia.org The Free
Enclyopedia

This account was recorded by a monk named Ralph from an abbot in England in the year 1200. It was written in *Chronicon Anglicanum.*

"In the time of King Henry II, when Bartholomew de Glanville was in charge of the castle at Orford, it happened that some fishermen fishing in the sea there caught in their nets a Wildman. He was naked and was like a man in all his members, covered with hair and with a long shaggy beard.

He eagerly ate whatever was brought to him, but if it was raw, he pressed it between his hands until all the joice was expelled. He would not talk, even when tortured and hung up by his feet. Brought to church, he showed no sign of reverence or belief. He sought his bed at sunset and always remained there until sunrise.

He was allowed to go into the sea, strongly guarded with three lines of nets, but he dived under the nets and came up again and again. Eventually he came back on his own free will. But later on he escaped and was never seen again."

John Norden – 1600

President Theodore Roosevelt and a Bigfoot Story

Theodore Roosevelt, Jr. was the 26th President of the United States. He was an American statesman and writer who served as the 26th President of the United States from 1901 to 1909. He also served as the 25th Vice President of the United States from March to September 1901 and as the 33rd Governor of New York from 1899 to 1900. As a leader of the Republican Party during this time, he became a driving force for the Progressive Era in the United States in the early 20th century. His face is depicted on Mount Rushmore, alongside those of George Washington, Thomas Jefferson, and Abraham Lincoln. – Wikimedia.com

Public Domain images of Theodore Roosevelt

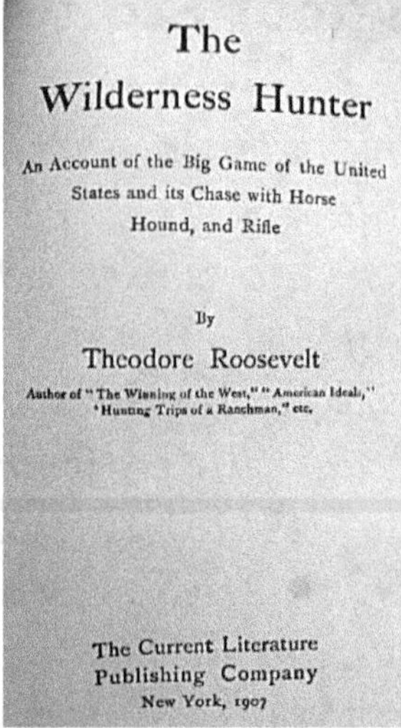

Excerpt from The Wilderness Hunter, 1893 (in public domain because of the time since publication).

"It was told (to me) by a grizzled, weather-beaten old mountain hunter, named Bauman,

who was born and had passed all his life on the frontier. He must have believed what he said, for he could hardly repress a shudder at certain points of the tales.

When the event occurred, Bauman was still a young man, and was trapping with a partner among the mountains dividing the forks of the Salmon from the head of Wisdom River. Not having had much luck, he and his partner determined to go up into a particularly wild and lonely pass through which ran a small stream said to contain many beaver. The pass had an evil reputation because the year before a solitary hunter who had wandered into it was there slain, seemingly by a wild beast, the half-eaten remains being afterwards found by some mining prospectors who had passed his camp only the night before.

The memory of this event, however, weighed very lightly with the two trappers, who were as adventurous and hardy as others of their kind... They then struck out on foot through the vast, gloomy forest, and in about 4 hours reached a little open glade where they concluded to camp, as signs of game were plenty.

There was still an hour or two of daylight left, and after building a brush lean-to and throwing down and opening their packs, they started up stream.

At dusk they again reached They were surprised to find that during their absence something, apparently a bear. had visited camp, and had rummaged about among their things, scattering the contents of their packs, and in sheer wantonness destroying their lean-to. The footprints of the beast were quite plain, but at first they paid no particular heed to them, busying themselves with rebuilding the lean-to, laying out their beds and stores, and lighting the fire.

While Bauman was making ready supper, it being already dark, his companion began to examine the tracks more closely, and soon took a brand from the fire to follow them up, where the intruder had walked along a game trail after leaving the camp. . . . Coming back to the fire, he stood by it a minute or two, peering out into the darkness, and suddenly remarked: "Bauman, that bear has been walking on two legs." Bauman laughed at this, but his partner insisted that he was right, and upon again examining the tracks with a torch, they certainly did seem to be made by but two paws, or feet. However, it was too dark to make sure. After discussing whether the footprints could possibly be those of a human being and coming to the conclusion that they could not be, the two men rolled up in their blankets, and went to sleep under the lean-to.

At midnight Bauman was awakened by some noise and sat up in his blankets. As he did so his nostrils were struck by a strong, wild-beast odor, and he caught the loom of a great body in the darkness at the mouth of the lean-to. Grasping his rifle, he fired at the vague, threatening shadow, but must have missed, for immediately afterwards he heard the smashing of the underwood as the thing, whatever it was, rushed off into the impenetrable blackness of the forest and the night.

After this the two men slept but little, sitting up by the rekindled fire, but they heard nothing more. In the morning they started out to look at the few traps they had set the previous evening and put out new ones. By an unspoken agreement they kept together all day and returned to camp towards evening.

On nearing it they saw, hardly to their astonishment, that the lean-to had been again torn down. The visitor of the preceding day had returned, and in wanton malice had tossed about their camp kit and bedding, and destroyed the shanty. The ground was marked up by its tracks, and on leaving the camp it had gone along the soft earth by the brook, where the footprints were as plain as if on snow! and, after a careful scrutiny of the trail, it certainly did seem as lf, whatever the thing bwas. it had walked off on but two legs.

The men, thoroughly uneasy, gathered a great heap of dead logs, and kept up a roaring fire throughout the night, one or the other sitting on guard most of the time. About midnight the thing came down through the forest opposite, across the brook, and stayed there on the hillside for nearly an hour. They could hear the branches crackle as it moved about, and several times it uttered a harsh, grating, long-drawn moan, a peculiarly sinister sound. Yet it did not venture near the fire.

In the morning the two trappers, after discussing the strange events of the last 36 hours, decided that they would shoulder their packs and leave the valley that afternoon. . .

All the morning they kept together, picking up trap after trap, each one empty. On first leaving camp they had the disagreeable sensation of being followed. In the dense spruce thickets, they occasionally heard a branch snap after they had passed; and now and then there were slight rustling noises among the small pines to one side of them.

At noon they were back within a couple of miles of camp. In the high, bright sunlight their fears seemed absurd to the two-armed men, accustomed as they were, through long years of lonely wandering in the wilderness to face every kind of danger from man, brute, or element.

There were still three beaver traps to collect from a little pond in a wide ravine nearby. Bauman volunteered to gather these and bring them in, while his companion went ahead to camp and made ready the packs.

Reaching the pond Bauman found 3 beavers in the traps, One of which had been pulled loose and carried into a beaver house. He took several hours in securing and preparing the beaver, and when he started homewards he marked, with some uneasiness how low the sun was getting.

At last he came to the edge of the little glade where the camp lay, and shouted as he approached it, but got no answer. The camp fire had gone out, though the thin blue smoke was still curling up wards. Near it lay the packs wrapped and arranged. At first Bauman see nobody; nor did he receive an answer to his call.

Stepping forward he again shouted, and as he did so his eye fell On the body of his friend, stretched beside the trunk of a great fallen spruce. Rushing towards it the horrified trapper found that the body was still warm, but that the neck was broken, while there were four great fang Darks in the throat.

The footprints of the unknown beast-creature, printed deep in the soft soil, told the whole story.

The unfortunate man, having finished his packing, had sat down on the spruce log with his face to the fire, and his back to the dense woods, to wait for his companion, …. It had not eaten the body, but apparently had romped and gambolled round it in uncouth, ferocious glee, occasionally rolling over and over it; and had then fled back into the soundless depths of the woods.

Bauman, utterly unnerved, and believing that the creature with which he had to deal was something either half human or half devil, some great goblin-beast, abandoned everything but his rifle and struck off a speed down the pass, not halting until he reached the beaver meadows where the hobbled ponies were still grazing. Mounting, he rode onwards through the night, until far beyond the reach of pursuit."

A Veritable Wild Man
Shared by Regina Headden

Tennessean – April 13, 1890. Bigfoot
A Veritable Wild Man

Chattanooga, April 12, 1890 Oakdale, Tennessee.

The people of Oakdale are very much excited over the coming and going of a veritable wild man, a compound of Sampson and Esau. Aprised by the appearance of a tall, broad shouldered man, naked from the waist up, with hair unusually long on his head, breast, and arms.

They began to guy him, when he threw one of them over an embankment and in a pitched fight which followed whipped six of his persecutors. A dozen railroad men finally overpowered and bound him ad locked him up in a fruit car.

Within an hour he was free, having burst the rope with which he had been tied and crushed the side of the car as if it had been paper. He undoubtedly escaped to the mountains and no anxiety to search for him is displayed.

For anyone pursuing historical accounts, the search of "wild man" will produce many results.

Photo from Ed Brown's Facebook Page – used with permission

An Interview with Ed Brown of Bigtruth

By Judith Victoria Hensley

(Ed Brown is well respected in the field of bigfoot research. He has conducted many investigations in eleven different states including, Washington, Oregon, California, Montana, Idaho, Ohio, Kentucky, Tennessee, Alabama, Florida, and Georgia. Not only has he conducted important research on his own but has also worked with some very qualified bigfoot researchers. Together, they have compiled a great deal of substantial findings.

One of the types of evidence he is involved in gathering includes recording of vocalizations that have long remained unidentified.

His organization, Bigtruth, is a team of investigators made up of Dan Lindholm and himself along with other investigators whom they invite to help with field research.)

Much of our investigating is conducted in southern Oregon which has resulted in a collection of significant evidence gathered from that state. Even though we have found many "structures" there, I am not really convinced by most structures. There are too many other natural ways they may be created such as snow fall, the heavy weight of ice, windstorms, and other natural events that break trees and cause branches to fall in different patterns.

Often people think they've discovered structures probably made by bigfoot, but closer investigation reveals them to be formations resulting from nature. When I see a suspicious looking structure in the woods, I don't just automatically say that bigfoot did it. I try to rationalize objectively according to the evidence.

On one occasion, we did find a tree structure that, in my opinion, absolutely could not have resulted by chance. There was no way in the world it could have happened naturally.

One particular log was probably forty-five or fifty feet long and two and a half feet in circumference. It was pushed down between two trees in a deliberate manner. It was a very heavy log. It had been jammed in between two trees and the evidence was the scuff marks that resulted from the action. Where bark had been rubbed against bark, it was easy to see that it had been pushed down, then jammed forward. It had to be moved twice to get it into place.

There is absolutely no doubt in the world that this is what had to happen to create the very distinct scuff marks in the bark. Even a group of guys could not have moved that log in such a peculiar manner. It would have been far too large and heavy, but a small group of bigfoot working together could easily have done it, whereas even big strong men could not.

On the *Bigtruth Youtube* channel, we post the results of our investigations including any video, audio, and things of that nature that we collect. We also have two shows. One show that I host is called *Sasquatch Encounters*. This is dedicated to my interviews with people who say they have had eyewitness sightings. They are given the opportunity to share their experiences. This is what I was doing when I heard all the reports of bigfoot encounters around Harlan

County, Kentucky, and prompted me to make the trip which resulted in my only personal eyewitness account of bigfoot.

The other show I do is called *Sit Down with Ed Brown.* On this show I interview more of the celebrity types. I've talked to Bob Gimlin, Jeff Meldrum, Cliff Barackman, and Adam Davies. The list goes on and on of the very well-known researchers I've interviewed in the bigfoot community. Both of these shows can be found on the Bigtruth channel on Youtube.

Ed Brown and Bob Gimlin

During research in the field, one of my favorite stories is known as the "Roll Call Incident." I was with four other researchers in the field. When it was time to come out of the woods, two came out and we assumed the others were still in the woods making their way out. Not knowing where they might be, I called out, "Roll Call!" which meant that if they were in hearing distance, they were supposed to answer loud enough for the other researchers to get an idea of who was still in the woods and how far out they were from the others.

Shortly after yelling out, "Roll Call," there was a response which I thought sounded like, "Here." I said to myself, "Okay, there's one."

The lady I was with saw a light way down in the woods in the opposite direction from where the verbal response had sounded. I said, "That must be Adam. The other two are still in the woods, but they're together, so they'll be fine. Let's go down and find Adam, since he's by himself.

We started walking that way and had gone down about half a mile and the light was coming back toward us. So, I assumed it was Adam walking back that way while we were moving toward him. When we met in the middle, it turned out to be one of the two I thought were still in the woods.

I asked, "Is Adam still back there?"

To my surprise, she answered. "Yes, they both are."

This meant there had been nobody from our research team in that section of isolated woods when I called "Roll Call." I had been recording during the incident and have it saved on audio. There is a clear response to my question. This is my favorite piece of evidence that I've recorded and have in my possession which offers proof. There were no other humans present. The entire research crew was way down in the forest in the opposite direction.

It was amazing. The recorder that we used for our research was set up really high with a big power box. It recorded sounds in a 360° circle, so it was capable of picking up sounds from any direction all the way around the recorder. On the recorder, on the opposite side from where we were and still very far away, there was a very clear, "Woop" sound. We did not hear it at the time it happened but discovered later when we were reviewing audio on the recorder.

So, not only did something respond to my yell for "Roll Call," but that was followed three or four seconds later with a very clear "Woop." That was a very cool, interesting piece of evidence. This recording is something we have not released publicly. The only reason is that I can't say definitively that it was bigfoot. I can't prove that's what it was. I still have the recording and if in my studies I discover another recording that sounds very much like it that is documented as bigfoot, then I will begin to release it. It was very cool.

I actually had an audio expert come in and clean up the recording to get a better, clearer response. When the response is amplified and cleared up, it sounds as if whatever responded to me was mimicking my voice. With my own ears I thought it said, "Here."

Ashley, who was with me, thought it said, "Yeah," but on the cleaned recording, it sounds as if it repeated, "Roll Call," back to me. What makes that interesting is that there are documented instances of bigfoot encounters in which the creature mimicked what it heard.

Researchers have considered the question of why they would mimic and have concluded that these creatures try to blend in with their environment. Hypothetically, if they know there are humans in the immediate area, they may mimic a coyote or an owl. There are lots of reports in the bigfoot community of owl sounds.

If mimicking is true, bigfoot could make the sound of an owl when humans were getting too close to them, to throw the humans off their pursuit. If humans believe they've heard an owl, they will not continue to investigate the sound in that area. The possibility is that they have learned how to communicate between themselves, even in an area with humans, without humans ever knowing they are present or suspecting they are using a mimicking sound to communicate with each other.

My bigfoot encounter took place in Harlan County, Kentucky on February 20, 2015. My brother, sister-in law, and I, based on several sightings I had heard about during my bigfoot research investigations, had made a trip to the area to check things out for ourselves. There were several stories that had been told about bigfoot sightings within a one hundred-mile radius of Harlan County, Kentucky. I found the accounts of eye witnesses very compelling and believed they were real because the descriptions of the creatures were identical in every case except one.

Every one of the eye witnesses said the creature they saw was about eight feet tall, with long hair on the shoulders. They observed little hair on the waist and on the legs. They did not say it was long hair. They described the being as dark brown in color, except for one account.

This lady said the creature she had seen was black, but she also said it was in the shadows. This would have obviously given it a darker appearance. I let that little discrepancy go because of the way the shadows would have impacted her perception of the coloring.

We were planning on going down from Cincinnati on February 20th of that year, but there was a snow storm predicted, so we decided to go down earlier and try to beat the storm. It was a horrible trip down. There was rain, ice, snow and a very bad travelling situation, but we went on down to Harlan. We got there and found almost a foot of snow on the ground.

Overnight it snowed even more. By the next morning, there was probably a good fifteen inches of snow on the ground.

I knew right away when I looked out of the cabin we'd rented the next morning that we were not going to get very far. Because of the terrain and the depth of the snow, it just wasn't going to happen the way we had planned. So, I went outside and took my binoculars with me. I was looking around in the woods for any kind of wildlife on the move that morning. Anything would have been easy to see against the backdrop of white snow.

I saw a trackway in the woods through the snow. I didn't know what had made the trackway, but something had, and I decided to follow it. It went up through the woods behind the cabin where we were staying. I could see the pathway clearly through the binoculars, but I wanted a closer look. I thought I would go on out and find that trail and follow it through the woods to see if I could figure out what had made it.

I started making my way through the forest. It seemed like at every turn there was a cliff, or the terrain was too steep, or something troublesome. So, I followed a little road around the mountain that looked like it went up to the top. I thought if I could follow it and get up the mountain, I could see the trackway from there and come back down the mountain to follow it.

I was literally on my hands and knees trying to climb the mountain. Under the snow were little logs, branches, twigs, roots, and loose rocks that couldn't be seen beneath the covering of snow. It is treacherous to try and walk on that kind of terrain in the snow. It is very easy to twist an ankle on something you don't realize is there. If you step on the edge of something or hit a hole that you don't know is there, it would be really easy to hurt yourself. The last thing I wanted to do was be out in the woods in the snowy, icy conditions and break an ankle.

I was going up the mountain carefully, on my hands and knees in places. All of a sudden, behind me I heard a very definitive, absolutely, positively the sound of a solid piece of wood hitting a solid piece of wood. In bigfoot research, this is known as a "wood knock," a thing that bigfoot has been known to do. It was very loud and very distinct. I froze there for a second, kind of thinking maybe I would hear it again, but I didn't.

After about twenty seconds or so I kind of turned around and was looking down at the snowy landscape. I took out my binoculars and was looking around at the other mountains to see if I could figure out what might have made that noise. To my surprise, I saw something walking down the side of the mountain quite a distance away, but in clear view in my binoculars. From that great distance, it was still a little small to my view, but there was no doubt about what I saw.

It was walking bipedally, down the side of this mountain. It had very long arms hanging down to its side. Its head was down, as if it was watching where it was walking. I couldn't make out how long the hair was or what color. I couldn't see defined details, but I could clearly see the silhouette. Whatever it was, it was walking down the side of the mountain, looking down as if it was watching where it was walking. It was having absolutely no problem whatsoever in its progress, while going through the same conditions as I was having to crawl on my hands and knees to get through.

That made it very impressive. It had to be a very large creature, a bipedal animal. I probably watched it clearly for about ten seconds. The funny thing was, and I find it psychologically very interesting as well, that I had a camera around my neck. Had I thought of the camera, I could have zoomed in and got a pretty good picture of the creature. I had a 200mm lens and could really have zoomed in and gotten a good picture of whatever it was.

However, during the time I was watching this creature moving across the snowy landscape with ease, I was wondering in my head what in the world I was looking at. I was trying to rationalize all the possibilities of what it might be.

Could it have been a man? I didn't think so because it was walking too easily in the snowy, icy terrain I was trying to get through on my hands and knees. I was so mesmerized and trying to consider the possibilities of what it was in my head that I actually forgot that I even had a camera! I didn't think about the camera. I didn't think about even taking a picture!

I was busy watching, trying not to miss anything or lose sight of that thing. There was a little patch of brush a few yards in front of the creature and I thought it would pass that way, go behind the brush out of my line of vision temporarily, but would come out the other side. That's when I finally thought of taking a photo. I got the camera ready and waited for the creature to come out the other side of the brush, back into view.

That didn't happen. Either it went behind there and stopped for some unknown reason or when it got there behind the brush, it turned and went down the mountain, following a path that was visually blocked from me. If there was one, it was going down the mountain on the other side. It would have been as if the creature made a ninety degree turn behind the bush and headed on down the mountain in that direction and the path was out of sight to me. Whatever it did, it never came out the other side of the brush as I had anticipated. I don't know where it went from there.

That's my story. It definitely was an interesting experience. In my own opinion, I believe I saw a bigfoot that day in Harlan County, Kentucky.

There have been other occasions when I thought I got a glimpse of something, but I couldn't be sure. Maybe, maybe not. If I can't say for sure about something, I will not try to convince myself or anyone else that what I've seen is bigfoot.

I can honestly say that I have never seen anything as clearly as what I saw in Harlan County. I've never seen anything else that I thought for sure was bigfoot besides that one incident. I've seen and heard plenty of signs, but that was my one definite visual sighting.

Facebook image of Ed Brown from his page

Bigfoot and the Johnny House
(reprinted from a former student project with Judith Victoria
Hensley at Wallins Elementary and Junior High in Harlan County,
Kentucky *Harlan County Memories*, 1995)
By K. Acelinger

A long time ago my mom lived back in the mountains. She said they had a Johnny House, just like the ones you hear about in the old days. That is another name for an outhouse.

One night she went out to the Johnny House and she heard something moving through the woods while she was in the outhouse. When she got out, she saw it but didn't know what it was. It was this big huge thing that looked like a man's shadow. When it got closer it looked like a big gorilla.

She went running back to the house. She said, "Mom, I saw something, but I don't know what it was!"

She told her mom that it looked like a gorilla. Her mom said it might have been a bear. Since her mother hadn't seen it, she had no idea what it actually looked like.

On a different night, my mom and her mother went out to the Johnny House together. When they came out, right there close by, she saw something that looked like a man's shadow. She said it was the same thing that she had seen before. That time her mother saw it, too!

They both ran back to the house and told Papaw Gilbert that they had seen something that looked like a man's shadow, but it looked more like an ape.

The next night they all went to the Johnny House together, taking turns. Papaw was the last one to go and mom and her mother had gone on back to the house. When he came out of the Johnny House and was walking back toward the house, he looked right behind and saw something that looked like a man's shape, but taller. It was hairy like an ape. It scratched my Papaw's face. He ran in the house. He still has the scars on his face.

Other people around the area saw it, too. Some people think it was Big Foot, but no one knows for sure.

Bigfoot in Dayhoit, Kentucky

(Reprinted from a previous student project with Judith Victoria Hensley at Wallins Elementary and Junior High in Harlan County, Kentucky)

By J. L. Graham, Jr.

I was about 15 or 16 years old when this incident occurred, and the year was either 1985 or 1986. It was a warm summer day. I had gone with Mom and Dad to visit my grandmother's house at Dayhoit, Kentucky. While they were talking, I decided I'd go walking up to the head of the holler. I planned to walk all the way up to the White Star Cemetery or as some call it – the Dayhoit Cemetery.

We're related to almost everybody in Dayhoit - the Tollivers, Griffeys, Williamses and all of them. My great-grandparents were Elijah Williams and Allie Kelly Williams.

I thought I'd walk up there to the graveyard just go to visit their graves and pay respects for a few minutes. Allie's dad was a stowaway on a ship from Ireland. They say there was no record of him ever signing in the ledgers at Ellis Island or anywhere else when he came to the United States because he was a stowaway. I was thinking about those things and really not much else, imagining their lives when they were young and coming over to America the way they did.

As I was walking along the road, I got an uneasy feeling like something was watching or following me. It was very peculiar. I had my thoughts on other things and that feeling just came over me suddenly and unexpectedly. The hairs started standing up on the back of my neck. I felt the presence of something, somewhere that I couldn't see.

I started looking around to try and spot whatever was setting off my internal instinctive alarms and causing the hairs on my body to stand up the way they were. I was trying to figure out what in the world was going on.

Then I got a glimpse of something out of the corner of my eye standing behind a tree on the side of the mountain, not far from the road (about 15 – 20 feet). At first it looked like a shadow, but as I continued to look, I realized that it appeared to be like a huge man about 6 – 7 feet tall. He was furry from the top of his head all the way down. His whole body was furry.

It seemed like he was watching me, or maybe had been following me up the mountain toward the cemetery. It didn't dawn on me right away that what I had seen for a few seconds might have been a Bigfoot. I looked down at the road for a second, and then looked back exactly where the figure had been a few seconds before. It was gone.

I can tell you, I was so scared it brought tears to my eyes! I ran from that point all the way to my grandmother's house where my mom and dad were visiting. I had run for over half a mile solid without even stopping to draw a breath. I was so nervous and crying, that I couldn't even tell what I thought I had seen for a while.

When I finally calmed down enough to talk and make sense, Dad and my uncle went with me back up the road to look for it or try to find some signs of it. I showed them exactly where I had seen it and tried to describe what it had looked like as best as I could.

It was so spooky and so surreal it scared the life out of me. I believe it actually happened. I saw bigfoot! You know, people will try to tell you that you must have just imagined a thing like that. To this day I remember it like it was still only yesterday. In my mind, it is still very real. If you were to ever see what I saw, it would be something you'd never forget.

The creature was covered in fur, dark brown and blackish looking. It was the middle of the day with the sun out and shining bright right on that big hairy man-like creature. It kind of looked like deer skin hide on it, like a mountain man would wear deer skin clothing or something but it was a little darker and a little lighter because of shadows hitting it.

It stood upright like a man and had hair all over its arms and legs - all hairy. There was no way to confuse it with a mountain man who might have had a big long beard. He would have had to be wrapped up in his own beard from head to foot if it was a mountain man.

I am a grown man now, and live in Bell County down by Calloway, Kentucky where the old Santa's Place used to be. I have heard about people who have seen something similar to what I experienced around the area where I live now. I am 41 years old now, and that happened when I was 15 or 16. I moved to Bell

County recently and am hearing stories of people seeing a very similar type creature right around here.

If I was in the woods, I'd never want to see that big hairy thing again by myself. Maybe if it was in a cage, I'd love to see it. It would have to be in a secure environment before I'd even want to go near it. I can tell you that I never again want to see such a creature out in the open like that.

I honestly believe the creature I saw was a Bigfoot.

I still watch on *The Discovery Channel* where people say they have seen a Bigfoot. My curiosity has been peaked about the subject ever since I had that experience to the point where I would love to talk to other people that know they have seen one – other enthusiasts and so on. I'd like to see what they'd have to say about what they saw, where they saw it, and how they felt when they saw it. I wonder if my experience was similar to theirs.

According to the *Discovery Channel*, the highest concentration of Big Foot sightings in North America is in Washington State, Canada, and in isolated locations around the redwood forests. The sightings they have reported and what that channel says on the topic is what I go by.

No matter if anyone else ever did believe me or not, I know I saw what I saw.

Free usage from Bigfoot Clipart

Yape Man and Yae-hoos
By the Late Ralph Harber
(Reprinted from a previous student project with Judith Victoria Hensley at Wallins Elementary and Junior High in Harlan County, Kentucky)

Our community sits on the Kentucky side of Brush Mountain and Stone Mountain, with Virginia on the other side. Rob Smith used to tell a big tale about someone seeing an ape type man in these mountains. He was supposed to be a big old black hairy man.

The old people called him a "yape." They told stories about him for the truth. Different ones claimed to have seen him around these mountains.

I never saw any such thing, so I really can't say. But just because you haven't seen something yourself doesn't mean that it absolutely isn't true.

People also used to tell their children that the big old black hairy booger man would come and get them if they didn't do as their mother and daddy told them to. Whether that was based on something people had seen or made up to scare children into being good, I don't know.

In Daniel Boone's journals when he was exploring this region of Kentucky, it is reported that he talked about killing a big hairy man-like creature that was supposed to be about 10 feet tall. Boone called them "yea-hoos."

It is not uncommon to hear an older mountain person refer to children as, "little yea-hoos."

Free Clip Art

An Encounter that Changed My Life
By Michael Cook

It was October 2000 that a strange event caused a fish called Walleye to run up stream in the river, and not for spawning purposes. The reason for the walleye's unusual behavior at that time is still undetermined to this day. Once I found out about the walleye, I was quick to ask my parents for a day off school to go fishing, promising any catch worthy of keeping I would bring home for dinner. They agreed, and I made plans to set out the next morning for a day on the riverbank. It was that day, on the side of the river, that suppressed feelings and fears would be brought back into light, and my life would forever change.

It was a perfect morning. The river was pristine, birds chirping, fish jumping, and the sun was peeking through the trees, burning off the fog that lay through the valleys. Not a care in the world for me, or for anything moving through the forest. I don't mean to brag, but the fish I was catching were all magnificent and I was quickly filling my bag limit.

For some time though, up on the ridge across the river, I heard a rustling that I quickly shrugged off as squirrels or birds playing. A few moments passed, and the rustling became noticeably louder and resembled footsteps of something heavy. This was the point at which I began to scan the ridge to discover what in the world was making such a racket. I heard limbs snap, then a low but loud groan.

This was followed by a crashing sound like a small car rolling toward the river through the underbrush of this steep hill. When it came into view, I saw a large ball of hair roll into the river, not fifty feet from me. I first thought it was a bear, so I dropped my gear, and got into position to flee in case this animal came up my side of the bank. I wasn't very far from my car.

Once it stood up, I knew this was something I had never seen before. It came up out of the water, its back toward me, wiping its eyes, and holding its long arms up out of the water. It waded toward the opposite side from where I was standing, took one step, with the aid of a small tree, pulled itself up on the five-foot ledge from where it had entered the water so violently.

It behaved like a big dog for a few seconds, shaking the excess water off its thick, dark brown hair. It began to maneuver back up on the steep hill, moving with grace and ease, like a ballerina would across a stage. It turned its head and that's when we locked eyes. My heart stopped and restarted, beating a hundred times faster.

I looked down as it brought its five fingered hands up and made fists. When it grunted loudly, I took that as my cue to run. My flight instinct had finally kicked in. I ran as fast as I could back to my car, leaving all my belongings lying on the ground. I knew this thing was chasing me down! I knew I was dead!

Once I made it to my car, I climbed in and locked the doors, looking every which way, positive the creature was near. I couldn't move from fear. I tried very hard to start the car, but all attempts failed. I wouldn't have been able to drive anyhow. My nerves were shot.

I started to calm down and came to the conclusion that the feelings I was experiencing were normal for what I had seen. They were feelings of sickness and lack of energy.

I cracked the window to let in air. That's when I heard the screams coming from up in the holler. They were a mix of a woman screaming and a growl all mixed into one. The sound was moving away from me. After thirty minutes or so, the screams subsided or had moved out of earshot. I quickly went back to the river bank and collected my gear, then went back to my car and left.

Back at home, I was tightlipped on what was clearly bothering me. My parents knew something was wrong but couldn't pin it down. Days, weeks, and months passed. Each night I would close my eyes and see this creature standing there. Its dark brown hair with hints of red in it, its skin weathered and black, its hands with five noticeable fingers balling into fists, its deep dark eyes looking at me as it turned its head in my direction. Whatever this thing was, it was definitely haunting me. Memories of the creature were not going away.

A full year passed after the encounter and I was still experiencing many sleepless nights. Then one night it all came clear. I was sitting with my dad in the living room, watching a TV show about Bigfoot. This particular show was talking about two men, Roger Patterson and Bob Gimlin, who had shot a video of a creature on a river bank, much like what I had seen.

Even though the creature I had encountered was different in many ways, the way the one on TV turned its head was the exact same way and movement that the one I saw made. The reality hit me like a ton of bricks. I had seen Bigfoot! There was no other explanation.

I went to my room and sat on the bed and began to cry. I cried because I had always thought people who claimed to see these creatures were either lying or completely crazy. I finally decided it was time to go back and try to figure out how big this thing actually was.

I arrived at the exact spot where I had my encounter, took off my shoes and waded out into the water. The ground on the ledge was still disturbed where this beast had fallen off and climbed back up. I waded to the exact spot, and the water was near my chin. On the creature it was barely below its chest, with another two and a half feet above the water. At that moment I knew this thing was at least eight feet tall, three feet across the back, and a whopping four hundred pounds at least.

There was no way it could have been a bear, or a person. I was and remain convinced that what I had seen is the creature known as Bigfoot.

Many years have passed since that day, and every day has been an adventure, and a journey that is far from over.

Michael Cook is a Bigfoot Researcher, Cryptozoologist and Author. Michael was born and raised in Southeast Kentucky, Harlan County. His encounter described in this story set him on a path of discovery. He has been researching sightings and encounters of unknown creatures for 17 years.

Michael has conducted authentic research in the field, interviewed eyewitnesses, and investigated sightings. He founded and led The Kentucky Sasquatch Team for five years, filing over 350 sighting reports in and around the state of Kentucky. He has since created **Cook Cryptid Research**.

His current focus is not only bigfoot research, but also other cryptid reports. He is currently doing his own investigations, collecting and cataloguing his findings, and contributing to the world of cryptozoology.

Public Domain Image

Ninja of the Woods
By Jimmy Blanton

I do a weekly podcast devoted to bigfoot eyewitness encounters and bigfoot research. I hear some pretty amazing stories from very sincere people.

One story I was told recently was from a lady in Loyall, Kentucky on Good Neighbor Road. She was fourteen years old at the time of the incident. It happened during the 1977 flood that wiped out so much of Harlan County.

The creature was outside her house. She described it as being dark brown and about seven feet tall. She wasn't sure what she was looking at out there, outside of her house, so she went out and shined a flashlight in the direction of the unidentified creature. It ran back up the hillside away from her and into the woods. She ran back in the house.

She says she heard "calls" for some time after. She believes she saw bigfoot.

If anyone has a story to share with me, or is interested in listening to my podcast, they can reach me at <u>bigjim392017@gmail.com</u> and on my podcast page, Ninjaofthewoods on Facebook.

If you're interested or curious about the unknown, then this podcast is for you. We discuss everything from Aliens, Bigfoot and other cryptids. Join me live on Saturday Night @ 9pm est

ninjaofthewoods@gmail.com

Photo by Judith Victoria Hensley

Daniel's Mountain Bigfoot

(Reprinted from a previous student project *Harlan County Memories*, 1995 with Judith Victoria Hensley at Wallins Elementary School and Junior High in Harlan County, Kentucky)

By C. Greene

This story probably happened about a hundred years ago at a place in Harlan County known as Daniel's Mountain. My great grandmother, along with many relatives and other men and women walked to church. That was their way of travel – walking or horseback mostly. This particular story happened in the fall of the year. They walked off the mountain and walked over into Wallins Creek to go to church.

After the church service was over, they had a long walk back home. It was very dark, and the wind was blowing. The women and children walked ahead, and the men lagged behind. One of the babies, which was my great uncle, was crying.

Mamaw said, "You men walk on ahead, so I can feed the baby."

There were no bottles or formula back then and she meant she needed to breastfeed the baby. Out of modesty, she would not do that in front of the men.

They went on up the mountain a little way and Mamaw found a big flat rock and sat down on it to feed Uncle Walter. She let him nurse for a while and everyone else had gone on ahead. She wasn't afraid because she knew they hadn't gone far, just far enough to give her privacy. There she sat in the dark by herself nursing the baby.

She heard something like sticks breaking when someone steps on them. It scared her. She thought it might have been a bear, a big cat, or something and the others had gone on ahead out of sight.

She felt something or someone staring at her. The baby stopped eating and started crying as if he knew something was wrong. She put the baby up on her shoulder and stood up.

When she turned around she saw a huge, hairy, black monster in the shape of a man. It was trying to take the baby from her arms. She screamed! She said the monster had eyes as big as saucers. She screamed again, and it ran away.

When the rest of the group heard her screaming, the men all came running toward Mamaw with lanterns and guns. She told them what had happened. They took the lamps and looked around a little bit. They could not find any sign of the monster.

Needless to say, they all wanted to get home as fast as they could. Whatever was out there in the dark had the advantage over them. There was no doubt that Mamaw had seen something that nearly scared her out of her wits.

The men looked for this monster from time to time after that, but they never could find it. They saw a few signs like big rocks that were turned over and tree limbs that would be broken, and big footprints in the sand or the mud. They never saw it again.

They decided to call the monster Bigfoot because of the size of the footprints. My great grandmother said the monster was probably as much afraid of her as she was of it. She never saw the creature again, but it was seen by other people on different occasions.

This is a true story that has been told over the years by my family.

Free use of image from Bigfoot Clipart

The Unsolved Mystery at Peabody
An Oral Interview with Bristol Belcher

(Mr. Belcher was the principal during the student book project at
Wallins Elementary and Junior High in Harlan County, Kentucky.
He currently serves at the Harlan County Board of Education. The
story is reprinted with his permission.)

My story starts about five years ago when
a buddy and I had gone hunting in Ohio
County, Kentucky. The place is called Peabody.
We had been there several days and had seen
nothing to kill. I had only seen a few does and a
couple of small bucks.

We were muzzle loading. My buddy and I
were hunting, and he was on the back side of
the ridge from where I was at. It was probably
seven or eight hundred yards across the top
separating us and he was still down on the
other side from me.

Like I said, I had only seen a few does those first several days of hunting. I had seen a couple of does come by that morning. The place where I was sitting was kind of at a river bottom with the river coming around it. Up on one side of the river, there was a thicket. There was a sort of ditch line that came up one side and ran up into the field where I was hunting. I was kind of over hunting some soybeans. It seemed like a good place to me.

I sat there until later in the evening. It was getting around 4:00 or 5:00 that evening and it was getting dark a little bit early. I looked down to my left. I saw someone or something standing down there. At first, I thought it was my buddy who is about 6'7" tall but what I saw wasn't him. Because he is so tall, he takes these big strides while he's walking in the mountains and it is really hard to keep up with him. I am not a tall person, and it is tough to keep pace with someone as tall as my friend who has such long legs. I have to take about two steps to keep up with his one.

I was just sitting on the cliff, watching. I saw some weeds move and kept watching, thinking that it could be a buck in the weeds. I kept my eye on it and waited a minute. I was sitting up on a cliff line that had come out of the bank. I didn't look away from that one that place where the movement was in the thick stuff growing by the river.

I caught a glimpse of something moving and at first I thought, "Well, I just saw it moving really fast and steady. There are no hops or jumps, just steady motion."

I looked down to my left and all I could see was what looked like somebody walking, taking huge strides. They were walking and covering a lot of ground very quickly, but not running. They just moved across the ground really, really fast.

At first, I thought it was my buddy with his big long legs. He covers a lot of ground. I really had just gotten a glimpse and not a good view of the person walking across the field. I got on my radio. We had CBs and we were talking back and forth.

I asked him, "What are you doing down here in front of me? Why are you walking up that river bottom? You know there is a thicket and you are going to run all of the deer out."

He said, "What are you talking about?"

I said, "Well, I just saw you walking out in front of me and I am looking at you right now. You're moving."

I never really could make out who or what was down there because it was kind of dusky dark, if you know what I mean.

I said, "What are you doing down here on this side?"

He said, "Are you joking? Are you trying to cut up? I'm actually dragging a doe right now."

He had shot a doe and was dragging it back toward me, toward the truck.

I said, "You have got to be kidding me!" He has a habit of time cutting up with people all the time, if you know what I mean. He loves to pull pranks all the time, and he's always doing this and that. I wasn't sure whether to believe him or not. Maybe he was just messing with me.

Usually, though, when we are out hunting, he is not one to do something silly because we all have muzzle loaders, rifles, and goofing off in the wrong place would be dangerous.

I walked down to the river bottom, kind of looking around to try and figure out what I had been watching. I wanted to find out what I had seen down there below me. By the time I got there, which was about 75 yards below me through the trees, I couldn't find anything. It was kind of muddy, and I looked for foot prints. I looked for anything and everything.

First off, I thought it was somebody else and I thought, "How would they get in there, because it's kind of hard to get in. You drive in. There's one lane; a big field, and there's a riverbank and the woods. It's all in the deep woods. There is no other way to get in there. You would have to swim that river, which nobody would do at that time of year. It was way too cold. Or they could walk in or drive in. If they would have walked or have driven in, I would have been able to see them come in to that field, either way. It had come from back to my left.

So, I'm not going to say what I thought it was because I really don't know. But it wasn't my buddy. He was actually dragging a deer at the time. I went over and finished helping him drag his deer to the truck. Today, I still can't even for the life of me figure out what I saw because there was absolutely no way of anyone getting in there to me the way the area was so isolated and blocked in by the river and the cliffs.

Whatever I saw was huge. My buddy is 6'7" tall. He is a big guy. The thing I saw was so big, I thought it was my friend. I surely thought it was him.

I would have had to keep a really crisp steady foot jog or I would not have been able to keep up with how fast that thing was moving through the woods. I really wish I could have gotten a better look at it to know exactly what it was.

It wasn't on all fours. It was on twos – on two legs. To this day my buddy and I still talk about it and he thinks I'm crazy.

I've never ever been out in the woods and seen anything like it before or since. That's my story. It's an unsolved mystery for me. Still to this very day, I do not know what was down there below me on the riverbank.

Public domain image from Pixabay

Was it Bigfoot?
By Opha Marie Hensley Jones

When I was a little girl, we lived in a house up in the Hensley Holler at Smith, Kentucky. The house was located by an apple orchard and had a creek running by the edge of the yard.

My mom and dad had bought a swing set for me and set it up in the yard between the house and the orchard. I loved that swing set!

I was very small, but I still remember most of what happened that day. My little brother, Byrd (or B.B. as we called him), and I were in the yard playing on the other side of the house away from the creek.

I heard something and looked across the yard to see a big black hairy thing standing on two legs by the place where we put our trash and burned it across the creek. It scared me to death. I didn't know what it was, but I knew I had never seen an animal like it before.

I was so young, I couldn't carry my little brother, but I was dragging him as hard as I could toward the house, trying to get us to the house and to safety. I was having a hard time, but I wasn't about to leave him out there with that thing, either. I was screaming for Mom.

By the time she came out to see what was the matter with me, and saw me dragging B.B. across the yard, the creature had taken off. They asked me if it was a bear.

It was not. I was sure of that. I did know what a bear looked like and that big hairy thing was no bear. It was standing on two legs in the creek, and was tall enough to be reaching from where it stood in the creek all the way over into the trash bin. It looked like a big black hairy man.

All these years later, I still remember seeing him standing there and as little as I was, I knew that I needed to protect my little brother and get us both in the house. I have never seen anything like it since then.

Sasquatch

(Reprinted from a student project with Judith Victoria Hensley at Wallins Elementary School and Junior High in Harlan County, Kentucky)

By C. Skidmore

It was a bright, sunny day and I was walking through Shane Mountain in Dayhoit, Kentucky which is in Harlan County. I was with my brother, C.J. We were walking through the woods, just walking around.

I heard twigs breaking, sort of like something big was walking in the woods, not too far away from us. C.J. heard the noise, too. We both started looking to see what was making all the noise. I thought it was my dog and that he had followed us up there.

I turned around and looked west of the trail and expected to see my dog coming through the leaves. We were up above my house. The crunching stopped when I turned around. About fifty yards away, I saw a big hairy creature that looked like it was seven or eight feet tall. It was standing right beside of a tree. We thought it was a bear at first, marking the tree.

It threw a rock at me! It threw the rock out of its hand like a human. I don't think a bear can throw a rock like that. I kept staring at it, thinking it had to be a bear, but that rock went right over top of my head, like somebody threw it at me. It threw a second rock while we were standing there staring at it, then it turned and ran away. It didn't get down on all fours like a bear. It ran like a man on two feet.

C. J. and I said to each other that we had better get out of there and get Uncle Matt. We ran home and told Uncle Matt, but he didn't listen to us. When I told him it threw a rock at me, he said, "Go to your room!"

"But... but... but..." I said. My brother didn't say a word.

"Go to your room and I will holler at you when supper is done. You must have seen a hairy man or a monkey that somebody let out. Ain't no such thing as a Sasquatch!"

Matt said, "Okay," and went on. I followed him. We decided there was no use of telling anybody if they weren't going to listen to us.

I wish he would have believed us, but he didn't and nobody else has believed it either. But my brother and I will never forget what happened.

Artwork by Craig C. Phillips – Washington State

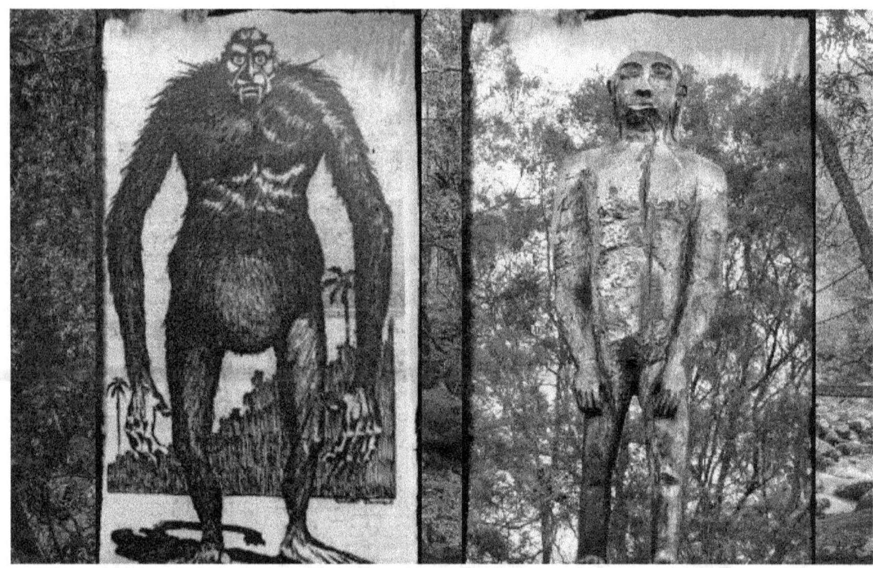

Left: A creature described by Australian surveyor Charles Harper, as depicted by artist Will Donald in the Sydney Sun in 1912. Right: A wooden yowie statue in Kilcoy, Queensland, Australia (Wikimedia Commons)

There's a Werewolf in My Yard

(Reprinted from a student project with Judith Victoria Hensley at Wallins Elementary School and Junior High in Harlan County, Kentucky)

Anonymous

A few years back people were reporting bears all over Harlan County. A lot of people were calling the Department of Fish and Wildlife to say they had a bear in their yard or had seen bear in unusual places where they didn't belong – like down town.

It kind of had people on edge.

One little woman called the police and complained that she had a werewolf in her back yard. They told her that there were no such things as werewolves.

She told them that the werewolf was about the size of a seven or eight-foot man, standing upright in her back yard. Of course, they thought it was a bear and told her to stay in the house and it would go away.

In a few minutes she called back and said that the werewolf was trying to come in on her. She said it was trying to tear the roof off of her house and come in. She was very frightened.

The officers went to check on her and try to figure out what was going on. She lived in a house, built kind of on a hill where one corner in the back was pretty close to the ground. She had put her trash bags up on that corner of her house, so the dogs and cats wouldn't get in them.

Whatever had been there had no problem reaching up and pulling those trash bags off the roof. More than likely it had been a bear. What she had heard that she thought was a werewolf trying to rip her roof off and get in her house had been an unidentified creature helping itself to her trash.

The officers tried to explain to her that it probably had been a bear and that they often get in human's trash looking for food. They suggested that she not keep her trash on top of the roof any more.

She still insisted that what she had seen was a big man, seven or eight feet tall, standing upright and covered in hair. She was so frightened it was obvious that she had really seen something.

It makes a person wonder, "Could the creature she saw actually have been Bigfoot?"

PD4 Pic Free Clip Art

Public Domain Images

A Lakeside Encounter
An Oral Story Told By Tony Felosi

(Tony in no stranger to the backroads of Harlan County. He traveled these roads all the time, every season, and every work day. He was in the woods constantly. For the last 7-8 years he has been employed by Harlan County, Kentucky doing property inspections or ordinance inspections. He is both an investigator and researcher of the unexplained. Cryptid research is only one area of interest for his artistic work. Tony is also a story teller, film producer and director.)

I have actually had two encounters. I can't tell you absolutely what it was, but I can tell you what it was not. It was NOT a bear. It was not a coyote, a coywolf or a wolf, like what are back in here now. I saw one of those two weeks ago at the bottom of Black Mountain.

This was the first encounter. I was with some people in Tennessee at a place called Greasy Hollow. We were there camping and fishing on Norris Lake. My dad and I were going to stay there two or three days, fishing, trot-lining, and camping. We had a few days off together and were just killing some time.

On the first night, there was some unusual stuff that happened with the pontoon. We had taken the pontoon from Blue Springs. It had taken us about two hours to get to the spot where we were camping way up the lake.

It had gotten dusky dark and we could hardly see. This was in the early 1980s and there were no other boats around us. There just wasn't a lot of boat traffic that far up the lake. We might have seen four or five boats a day. If a boat was approaching, we would have heard that very easily.

For no reason known to us, our boat started rocking. It wasn't a little bit of motion, but really kind of violent. It wasn't enough to have turned the boat over, but it was enough that the pots and pans were clanging. We did our cooking on the boat and had a gas stove and our cooking utensils.

There was no boat in sight. I don't know if it might have been a big swell from something or not, but it was a continuous motion. We also didn't know if there was something out there that didn't want us there.

It was very unusual, to say the least. Dad had been on the lake a whole lot longer than I had, but I had been spending a lot of time there. When you've been in the same place on the lake a lot of times, you get very familiar with it. You know the ebb and flow, the night noises, and everything normal for the location.

There had been no boat motor, nothing like that to create a wave strong enough to violently rock our boat. We kind of wrote it off, though, convincing ourselves that maybe there was a boat on the far side of the lake and we just hadn't heard the motor because we were talking or something.

Late, late that same night behind the tent we heard something breaking trees. It sounded like something was breaking saplings, smacking wood, and such. A lot of bigfoot researchers talk about wood knocking, which is the sound of a piece of solid wood hitting another piece of solid wood. We definitely heard those kinds of noises. Neither one of us had ever heard that before.

Some of the old timers, like guys who worked in the mines, and didn't have a real big sense of humor told tales. With them it was all about survival. They worked hard, took care of their families, and sometimes got to go fishing on the week-end. These guys were nice guys, but they were kind of hard. Most of them had been raised during the depression and started to work in a coal mine at the age of 13 – 15 years old. This is the kind of hardened older guys I mean by old timers.

They would tell stories about strange encounters in the woods, like something unseen that would throw rocks at you. They also talked about something beating the trees, jumping on top of a boat and jumping back off. Some of them had houseboats they'd take up the lake. Several of them swore that something would jump on top of their houseboats while they were trying to sleep. They could often hear it walking around on top of the boat, but when they'd go out to try to find out who or what was up there, it would be gone. It would have taken something big, actually quite large, to rock a houseboat, or be heard walking around on top like that.

These men also told stories of being anchored off fishing and having something throw rocks at them from the cliff line. Whatever was up there wasn't necessarily trying to sink their boat, but was definitely trying to scare them off. When the big rocks started hitting the water, it would ruin their fishing and they would just pull up anchor and go.

Whatever it was in the woods along the lake that didn't want people there had learned certain behaviors to get a response from the humans. If they did something like breaking saplings, rocking boats, or throwing rocks in the water to scare the fish away, then the people would leave.

Those are some of the tales I've heard from the older generation who spent time at the lake.

One time we actually heard a "screech" from the woods nearby where we were anchored. It is a sound that once you hear it, you will never forget it. It was kind of a cross between a woman screaming and a growl, but much deeper than a woman's scream. It was a very primal, guttural type of scream. That kind of threw us for a loop. Neither of us had ever heard such a sound before.

Bears don't do that. Panthers and mountain lions scream, but they don't push over trees. Neither one can throw rocks.

The next day, I tried to go out and find footprints. I didn't find any, but I did find where the trees had been messed with. The whole thing kind of unnerved us a little bit.

The next night, this thing started screaming again. It did that for a while, then shook the trees and snapped them like they were dried branches.

In the middle of the night it sounded like it actually got up in the trees and began making these really weird guttural noises and screams.

A mountain lion is not going to go up a tree and act like that, and neither will a bear.

As close as the screams sounded, you would have thought we'd be able to see something. We could hear it for sure, but we could not see it.

We had to "sleep with the lights on" so to speak. We became very apprehensive, but finally dozed off and were both getting a little sleep. Then, I'm telling you – right behind the tent this thing screamed and almost literally shook the tent. It was that loud.

We thought it was going to come through the tent on us. We didn't have any defense except a pea shooter, a little six shooter, a hatchet, and a hunting knife. We expected to be attacked at any moment.

Then we decided that we should not go outside the tent. We thought that maybe if we just stayed very quiet and stayed inside the tent without any kind of reaction from us, it would move on.

It raised a ruckus for probably fifteen or twenty more minutes and then just left.

After it came daylight the next day, we loaded up all of our stuff and left. Something obviously didn't want us there and we didn't want to be there any longer!

The only time I ever heard anything even similar to that was years later at Yancy. I've heard bears and wolves before. I know what they sound like.

I was turkey hunting in the fall, in the fog. I had been doing some turkey calls, and heard some turkey responding. I was easing down the mountain.

Probably 50 or 60 yards away, I heard it and heard it echo. I couldn't tell exactly where it had come from because of the way the fog was lying. It was a very similar sound to what we had heard those nights on the lake. It was a very very guttural, growling sound.

I had a very strong sensation that I was being watched. I don't know if it was hunting me or maybe just trying to intimidate me and let me know it was there. It did not throw anything. I heard three or four growls, pretty close to me, but that was it. I got out of there.

I've thought it through many times, both incidents. I don't know what made that kind of noise. Maybe it was this, or maybe it was that. Maybe it was a coyote. I've had a lot of experience in the woods, but I couldn't identify the sound as anything I'd ever heard before except on those two occasions.

It was very unusual. There were not a lot of bears back then, but there were some. If you got too close, they would "woof" at you, or shake the bushes. I knew what that was. I'd seen plenty of bear tracks.

I can't explain either one of those encounters. I can't say that it was a sasquatch. I can't say that it wasn't. I honestly still don't know what it was and can't explain it.

Drawing by Brian Ingermann

(Brian Ingermann is an award-winning cartoonist, caricature and an IMDb storyboard artist from Indiana. He originally grew up in the Ouachita Mountains of Hot Springs Arkansas and began drawing in 1972.

He is a USAF Veteran and was awarded the 1985 USAF Cartoonist of the year for work completed on the base newspaper. He has a formal art education from The Art Institute of Indianapolis, Sinclair College in Dayton Ohio and The John Herron Institute of Art in Indianapolis.

He completed storyboards in September of 2017 for the Stephen King Film The Man Who Loved Flowers based on a short story in King's Night Shift Collection. He currently has a contract to do art for Bad Anger Pictures which is owned by Actor Dan Yeager and his Producing Partner Writer Ron Scott.)

North Carolina Bigfoot

(Reprinted from a student project with Judith Victoria Hensley at Wallins Elementary School and Junior High in Harlan County, Kentucky)

By C. Carmical as told by Lance Carmical

My cousin Lance is a long-distance truck driver. A while back he was driving home from work in North Carolina on Highway 20. It was about two or three o'clock in the morning. All he had on his mind was getting home.

He saw something ahead in the road just beyond what his headlights would show clearly. It stood still staring at the oncoming lights. When he got close enough, he realized it was a creature standing right in the middle of the road!

He stopped a little way back. It was staring straight at him with the headlights hitting the creature and revealing it clearly in the light. There were no other cars around or people. For a few seconds in time their eyes were locked together on that empty road.

Lance was so shocked, he just sat there staring. The creature turned away from him. There was a long tree standing on a bank across the road. The creature took long strides across the road toward that tree. Then it turned back and looked at him one more time before it grabbed that tree and swung up the hill and out of sight. The creature was so strong, when it grabbed hold of that tree to pull itself up it almost pulled the whole tree out of the bank.

He said he has never seen anything like that creature in his entire life before or since that incident. He estimated that the creature stood about six and a half feet tall, or maybe even taller than that. It had a brownish, grayish color of hair all over its body. Lance said it was more brown than gray.

There were no other cars around on that road at that time in the morning. It shook him up so badly, he didn't know what to think about the whole episode. He drove straight on through to home, thinking about it the whole time.

He told his dad, "Dad, you might not believe me, but I think I just saw bigfoot when I was driving through North Carolina on Highway 20!"

His dad could tell by the way it had shaken him up that he definitely had seen something out of the ordinary. From the way he described it, it could very well have been bigfoot.

Lance says that is one thing he has seen and experienced in his life that he will never, ever forget. He said he was scared that everybody would think he was crazy if he told them he had seen bigfoot. It took him a long time to be willing to tell his story to anybody else because of that. We appreciate him sharing his story with us for this book.

Photo by Judith Victoria Hensley

Artwork by Brian Ingermann

Bigfoot Research

An Interview with Thomas Marcum

Thomas Marcum is the founder/leader and webmaster of the cryptozoology research organization known as The Crypto Crew. He has over 20 years of experience with research and investigation of unexplained activity, working with video and websites, and is certified in Dreamweaver. He is a nature and wildlife enthusiast with many years of experience hunting and fishing. He's also a trained wild land firefighter, and a published photographer, author, film maker, and poet.

I have seen bigfoot. This was in the very late fall of 2016 or the very early part of 2017 during the winter. There was a white snow on the ground. I live in the mountains, up a hollow like most people in this area. If I look out my front window, all I see is mountains, and if I look out the back window, all I see is mountains.

There was a light snow on the ground and I was pretty bored in the house. I was looking out the window to see if anything was going on outside. That's when I saw a creature that I believe was a very large bigfoot.

It was in back of my neighbor's house. I watched it step in between two trees. It walked to the right just a little bit as it walked that way. There were some smaller trees there that still had their brown, dried up leaves on. They kind of hid the creature a little bit as he passed through that spot. If might have walked for fifteen feet to a place where there was a little dip going up the holler and up the mountain. After it got there I couldn't see it anymore.

This is the clearest sighting I've had with no obstructions in my line of vision initially when I saw it come between the trees and walk in the open for several feet. I got a very clear look at it. This thing was humongous! It was dark in color.

My theory as to why it was there is because this neighbor always put out scraps, or at least used to, to feed the coons, bears, or whatever else might be having a hard time getting food in the winter. I think that because the winter was pretty hard that year. The creature had come down to that area trying to get an easy meal.

When it stepped in between the two large trees, a red oak and a poplar, I didn't realize how big it was until a few days later. I saw my neighbor, who is a six-foot tall man, standing right in the spot where I had seen the creature. He mows his grass in the summer and keeps things cleared away back to that level of his property. He was standing back there, and the creature had been much taller than this man. It must have been ten feet tall.

I have been researching bigfoot for over twenty years. I've found numerous tracks, heard them make sounds, and found numerous stick formations. I've probably talked to over a thousand eyewitnesses in interviews and research I've conducted. I'm convinced for sure that bigfoot is real.

I have written a book called *Bigfoot Witness*. In that book, I have documented a lot of the sightings in Bell and Harlan Counties, and also others from around the United States and Canada. *(This book is still available through Amazon, Barnes and Noble, and Walmart.com It is also available on the website Crypto Crew.com)*

From the accounts I've gathered in this area, the average height of a bigfoot is between six and seven feet tall. The predominant color is always black, but I do have reports of reddish ones and some white ones.

Right now, there seems to be a lot of bad information being put out for some unknown reason. This is unfortunate, because bogus reports and hoaxes undermine the validity of true sightings.

I can tell you about the experience that converted my dad. It's a great story.

My dad never did believe in bigfoot. In fact, over the years, he had ribbed me a little bit and poked fun at me for researching bigfoot and following bigfoot reports and things.

He came over to my house one day in 2013. At the time he was having some pretty bad heart problems.

When he said to me, "Come out here. I want to talk to you," my immediate thought was that it had something to do with his heart. Maybe he had gotten a bad report from the doctors that he wanted to tell me about.

We went out on the back porch and sat down. He said, "Well, I've seen a bigfoot."

I said, "You've seen a what?"

He repeated the statement. "I've seen a bigfoot."

He told me where he had seen it. "It walked right across the road in front of me and it was only about thirty feet in front of my car."

I said, "Dad! Why are you just now telling me?" (It was about five days after the sighting.)

He said, "Well, to be honest, I've made fun of you over the years and I was ashamed to come and tell you that I actually saw one myself!"

I said, "Will you take me over there to where it happened? I want to look for myself and see."

The sighting happened early in the morning. The reason he was out that early was because he was going to pick up my cousin who was on night watch duty at a coal mine nearby, a deep mine that was temporarily shut down.

He took me back to the spot and showed me where it had crossed the road. Right where it had crossed the road, there was a foot track beside of the road.

It was a two-lane road with a double yellow line going down the middle. Dad said, "It took two steps, and it was almost across the road. By the third step, it was hitting the grass on the other side."

I looked around and on the other side of the road, not right on the edge, but further away from the road, I also found some tracks, a little bit off at the edge of the mountain. It was getting late in the evening, so we left and I came back the next day. Actually, I went back to the same spot several days in a row.

I was able to find over thirty tracks in one line. Altogether, I found around one hundred tracks in that area. Of course, I followed the tracks and found where it had broken branches and where it had made the stick formation that looks kind of like a teepee. Sometimes they make "Xs" with wood and I found some of those in the area.

What made the creature walk out in front of my dad, or what I believe, is that where the road is, it comes into a "T" formation where the car has to turn right or turn left. If you look to the right, you really can't see up the road to see what's coming. As my dad was coming off the mountain, to the place of the T-junction, he had to swing the car to the right to see what was coming on the road, but he was actually going to turn left.

When he did that, the bigfoot walked out in front of him. My train of thought is that the creature actually thought he was going to turn to the right and stepped out. When my dad turned left instead, the creature was already in the road. Dad was going very slow, as a person does when they've come to a stop and then going to pull out.

Dad said the thing was big enough that it could have torn his car all to pieces if it had wanted to. He never did believe in bigfoot, or ghosts, or anything like that. He just didn't believe in that kind of stuff. After his own encounter, he did!

I got a really good plaster cast of a clear footprint among those around the site where my dad had seen bigfoot. I wish I had made more, but to cast them all would have cost a fortune! I still have the one that I cast. I have pictures of it. The track itself was thirteen inches long, but the unusual thing was that at the ball of the foot, it was seven inches wide.

I am a big guy. I'm almost 6'4" tall and my foot is only five inches across at the ball. This happened in July. I weigh 300 pounds without a backpack. That day I had on a backpack and I walked in the same place he walked. There were a lot of pine needles and the ground was a little bit soft. You can sink up in them a little bit. The impression from the bigfoot was pressed down at least twice as deep as my feet.

Based on that, I estimate it to have been at least six hundred pounds, if not more.

One day when we were out in the mountains he told me, "Seeing bigfoot has ruined me. Now, I can't go out in the mountains to do anything without looking for signs of bigfoot, whether it's a track or whatever. It has totally ruined me!"

I am in the woods a lot, myself, and I'm always looking for signs of things that are peculiar and out of place. I did logging for a long while and you get used to the "normal" environment. You know what it looks like when a tree falls and gets uprooted. You know what the natural breaks and scrapes look like. You learn what is a natural fall and can spot things that look unusual.

My dad and I used to coon hunt years ago. We would mark our path in the woods by breaking a limb and pointing it in a certain direction. I think that's pretty common among hunters or people who don't just hike on trails that are already well marked. They will break a limb in a certain direction to mark their trail. I think bigfoot may do the same thing. If you see a branch ten feet up that has been broken and twisted for no obvious natural reason, it makes you wonder. If you find several of them in a direction, you really have to wonder.

I actually caught this thing on one of my game cameras in the same area where my dad had the sighting and I found the footprints. I was trying to document everything, so I went in and set up a game cameras in the area, hoping to get a shot of something.

Photo from Game Camera – Thomas Marcum

While I was doing that, I heard a weird sound, like somebody talking. It was just far enough out of earshot to not be able to hear what they were saying, or at least I couldn't make out any words. It spooked me. At first, I thought maybe it was my dad coming to check on me because I was by myself. At that time, I didn't even pack a gun with me or anything else for protection when I went out in the mountains.

I kept hearing what sounded like talking. Even though it scared me, I wanted to put the game camera up right there anyhow. I got it set up right by where I found the thirty tracks in one line. After I got all that done, I cleared out and came home. My mom and dad weren't even home.

I am under the assumption that I was in his territory and that was the bigfoot following me. I had been talking to the camera and I believe the bigfoot was mimicking me. I think it was trying to mimic what I was saying. There are other reports of them doing this mimicking.

I went back about thirty days later to get my game cameras from the area. I looked at the photos they captured. I got one that was kind of overexposed. The next one was also overexposed, but there was a figure standing there. Of course, it was like 3:00 in the morning when the camera snapped the photo, so the picture was overexposed. It is hard to see a great amount of detail, but it is easy to make out a head, a torso, and a right arm that appears to be very muscular. I included this in one of my films.

I went back later and stood in the spot where it had to be standing for the position in the picture in relation to the camera. The creature would have had to be more than six foot tall, but not over seven feet tall.

Photo by Thomas Marcum

I have found a lot of signs in that area. I found a teepee structure in the exact same area, where there had not been one before. I went back a few days later and more sticks had been added to the original one. I documented the changes for over three years. Over that length of time, more sticks were added to the structure. I also found foot tracks within ten feet from the teepee with the prints leading toward it.

One day I went in there and went back to check for any more changes to the structure and it had been completely torn down and gone.

These are just a few of the many experiences I have had personally with bigfoot. I've talked to many, many people who have had experiences with bigfoot. I've been doing this for a long time.

I've also done quite a bit of debunking. A lot of time people will have a really hard time with tracks because they don't really know wildlife. Sometimes a bear track will fool them. A bear's hind foot will sort of step into the edge of its front foot sometime and it will make it look like a ten or twelve-inch track. If you aren't really experienced with tracks, it would be easy to mistake that for something else. I've seen that kind of bear track really fool good researchers.

I can't imagine why anyone would deliberately try to falsely report a sighting or pass off a fake foot track. Maybe they do it for attention, to get publicity for themselves, or maybe hoping for some kind of monetary gain. I don't know. I don't get it.

When someone has really seen one, it is not hard to tell that they have really seen something. It will shake a person up. I have a neighbor, Terry Roark, who had a sighting right down below my house about a fourth of a mile away. It really shook him up. He has actually had two encounters.

Terry lives right across the road from me. One of the bigfoot sightings that he had, I was behind it by about two hours when I interviewed him. My dad called and told me, and I went to talk to Terry.

"I hope I never see one again!" he told me. He was pretty shaken.

Years before he had seen one up the road at a place known as Dead Man's Curve. He saw one in the creek there. Terry does some of his walking on the railroad tracks. He saw the creature splashing in the water in the creek near the railroad tracks. After I talked to him, I tried to back track from his sighting to the creek area and found an "X" that seemed to be freshly made. It was from one chunk of wood that had been torn in two instead of two round sticks. It looked as if it had been freshly torn apart and laid the "X" in the fork.

Where he saw the other one was right below my house, up on the hill where some members of my family live. They were telling me about the dogs they kept back there and their food. They saw a bigfoot back there. It happened back in the 1970s probably. They are both dead now. They thought the creature might have been trying to get to their dog's food.

The Shacklefords lived across from me. Walt had come down to my house and wanted me to look at his computer. At that time, I was doing a little computer work.

He told me, "There is something behind my house. I don't think it's a bear."

Since we were having so many encounters in the area, I said, "It could possibly be a bigfoot."

He said again, "I don't think it's a bear. It's too big."

At that time, they had a really old dog living up at their house with hardly any teeth. It was a bird dog. They fed it in a little pan next to its house. I thought if it was a bigfoot, it might be coming in there and taking the dog's food, unafraid of the dog. So, I went up there to look. By their house we found some freshly broken trees that were about two inches in diameter. They were broken and pushed under an old dead log that had been there so long that it was growing moss on top. I also found what looked like a bigfoot track there, but it was partly washed out. All of that was about fifty or seventy-five yards from where I had seen the bigfoot step out from between the two trees.

All of those things took place within a year or two. Also during that timeframe, we would hear things in the mountains at night, like something big was moving through the brush, but we never could see anything because the landscape on the mountain was dark.

I was not a part of a bigfoot community in the beginning. I did the study and research on my own. I didn't think anything about information being on the internet. I just started that back about 2011, putting things up on the internet. I didn't even realize the bigfoot community was so big. There are a lot of people interested in this subject.

Photo by Judith Victoria Hensley

Appalachia offers terrain, fresh water, and plenty of food sources for bigfoot and other elusive creatures to thrive.
– Judith Victoria Hen

The Big Hairy Monster

((Reprinted from a student project with Judith Victoria Hensley at Wallins Elementary School and Junior High in Harlan County, Kentucky -*Harlan County Memories – 1995*)

By C. Greene

Once there was a man who had a big black cow named Mary. One cold dark night she did not come home, and he went out to get his cow. He couldn't find her, so he went on back to the house.

The cow had a big bell around her neck, so he could hear the bell ring and find the cow by that sound if she was too stubborn to come to him. He heard the bell, so he went looking for the cow again. He found her down at the lake below Molly Daniel's house.

He got his cow and put her on a rope to lead her home. The cow started bawling. She did not want to go with him. At first, he did not know what in the world was the matter with her. She was usually a gentle cow. He pulled and pulled on the rope, but Mary wouldn't come.

Finally, he was fed up with trying to get her to come. He got so aggravated at her he decided to tie her to a bush and leave her there until morning. After he had her tied up, he turned around to head home and came face to face with a big hairy, ugly monster! It was standing upright like a man and was hairy all over. The hair looked greenish in the moonlight.

The man ran one way and the monster ran the other.

He left the cow tied to the bush and ran home to get his big long hunting rifle. He went out looking for the monster. He saw it again and fired a shot at it but missed. It took off running and no one ever saw it again.

After that, that old cow, Mary, got to where she would go home with the man without any trouble. She never did run off to that lake again. She just stayed around home with her bell around her neck.

Bigfoot Stalker?
By Franklin Smith
(Reprinted from a student project with Judith Victoria Hensley at
Wallins Elementary School and Junior High in Harlan County,
Kentucky)

I used to live in Smith, Kentucky when I was a teenager. I loved the mountains and my friends' and I were all over the place on dirt bikes, hiking, or camping out. We were happy in the mountains running around free.

We used to go to Bible Study at Ernest and Gladys Hensley's house one evening a week. Afterwards, we'd all walk each other home. My cousin, Donna Smith, lived the furthest up the road. So, we'd all walk her home first, and then drop other people off on the way back down the road until we got everybody delivered safely home.

One night we didn't have the usual crowd walking people home after Bible Study. Donnie Smith, Donna Smith, Larry Ray Eldridge, our Bible teacher, and I had walked up the road that starry night to drop Donna off at her bridge. We would stand on the main road and watch until we saw her go safely on her porch and in her front door.

That night it had seemed like something was walking with us, or walking parallel to us through the fields, gardens, and underbrush beside of the road. We would hear something every once in a while, and it made us a little uneasy. It might have been a stray dog, a deer, or even a bear, but we were making plenty of noise, and there were lots of houses along the main road. We weren't too scared.

All of a sudden something let out this gosh awful sound somewhere between a scream, a growl, and a howl that absolutely made the hairs stand up on the back of our necks. We froze in our tracks. None of us had ever heard anything like that before in our lives. It was a mixture of sounds, and it wasn't very far away, maybe a hundred yards or so.

We turned back down the road and knew not to run, but we sure laid down some tracks, sticking close together as we went. It shook us all up.

Of course, we never did know for sure what it was, but it sounded big and very, very loud. There were no other sounds around it, no answering calls, or any sounds of an animal fight – nothing. The closest thing to that howling, yowling, growling scream that I can think of are some of the recordings that people have and say they are from bigfoot.

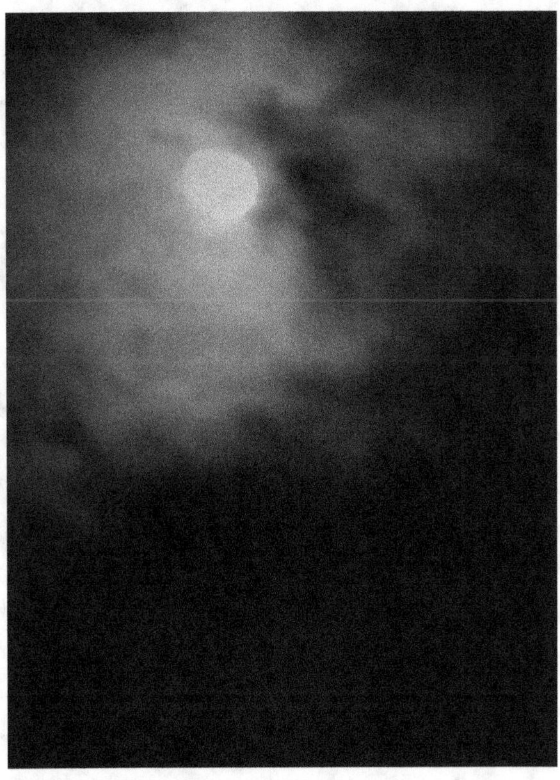

Image by Brian Ingermann

Similarities Between Cryptid Sightings and Bigfoot Sightings

By Ed Brown

There are actually many similarities between what bigfoot researchers go through and what people who have seen black panther, big cats, or have encountered other cryptids when they share their stories. The similarities are actually very close.

It is a shame that people's stories are devalued and not believed when they adamantly report having seen something. There are a lot of credible people having credible experiences with not only panther and big cat sightings in the Appalachian region, but also throughout the entire country that we run into while doing bigfoot research.

Those valuable witnesses are ridiculed because the people who don't believe them have an attitude of, "Oh, you didn't see that! You didn't see what you think you saw!"

In my bigfoot research when I've come face to face with these attitudes, I want to know the answer to this question. If bigfoot isn't real, or even black panther for that matter, how is it that so many witnesses are seeing them? The word of hardworking people ought to be enough.

In the middle of the eyewitness accounts are lawyers, judges, teachers, police officers, and doctors – all who have been trained in their profession to be very observant and concise in details of what they've seen. These professions are trained to think critically and be sure of what they saw.

People who live close to the land such as farmers, hunters, woodsmen, and campers are also very much aware of what is around them. They are unlikely to mistake one animal for another. While they are working the land or in the great outdoors, they are constantly aware of the things of nature around them.

So many people have reported sightings of bigfoot that we must conclude one of two things. Either bigfoot is real, or there is some mass delusional psychosis going on which would convince people from all walks of life and all around the globe to report bigfoot encounters. All of these peoples are not lying. They simply are not.

Are there people among the reports who are lying? Absolutely. There are hoaxers. There are people who want fame and want to get their name out there. They don't care to lie about an encounter, to try to get famous or draw attention to themselves. It does happen.

But is this the motivating force behind every individual that reports a bigfoot encounter? Absolutely not.

The scientific odds of every single person who says they've seen bigfoot being a liar is not only improbable, but impossible. For every single individual to lie about what they've seen and give eye witness accounts to the physical characteristics that are so similar, or the behaviour or smell of the animal being described so precisely by so many different individuals across the United States and around the world is impossible.

If you took every sighting in the world of bigfoot over the years and said that 99.99999% of them were liars, that would still leave the .00001% that is telling the truth. There are hundreds of thousands, if not millions of reports of bigfoot (known by many different names) from around the world. That doesn't account for all the encounters and sightings that are never reported or never documented for one reason or the other. It doesn't include the people who are afraid to share their encounter because they don't want to be laughed at, scoffed at, or accused of lying.

If only 1 out of every 10,000 sightings is real, it still makes the animal real. People are seeing something on every continent that fits the description and behaviour of what we commonly call bigfoot in the USA.

Every single state in the United States, besides Hawaii has reports of bigfoot. That being said, if we are looking at a specific region like Appalachia, research is being conducted in a much narrower area. Any sighting of any animal or report of any cryptid should be taken seriously unless debunked by an objective researcher.

When a report is made, somebody with a scientific investigative background should at least go out and talk to the individual, listen to their story, try to find supporting facts, and document the details of the story for a data base.

I Never Want to See it Again!
By Terry Roark

I can share two incidents about seeing bigfoot. They are both very real to me, even though time has passed.

One happened about three years ago down below my house at a curve. It was in October 2013. I was coming back up the road toward home after being out for a walk and a big hairy creature came out of the bushes. It slung its arms and headed up in the mountain.

I thought to myself, "What in the world is that?" I had never seen anything like it before in my life. I'm used to the mountains and I've seen a lot of animals, but I surely had never seen anything that even came close to resembling that big black thing!

It was a big black creature walking on two feet and covered in hair. When it went up the mountain, on a very steep incline, it was walking fast and flat-footed without a bit of trouble up that place. I can tell you that no man could have walked that fast and that easy up something that steep. It didn't make any noise either.

The other time, I was walking up the railroad tracks. I often do that for my evening walks. I heard something splashing in the creek and looked over toward the creek where the noise was coming from.

There was a big black hairy creature again that looked like the other one. It may have been the same one. I don't know, but it was years apart. It was splashing around in the creek.

When it saw me, it turned and ran up in the mountains. It didn't have any trouble at all going up the bank or up into the woods. It didn't have to grab a hold on anything to pull up, or anything at all. The animal made it look very easy, and it was not an easy place for a human being to move that fast, I can tell you that!

It really scared me! I took off at a trot. Again, I thought, "What in the world was that?"

I'm guessing it was about six-foot tall and broader through the shoulders than a regular person would be. Also, it had longer arms.

I told my cousin Charlie about it and he said, "You saw a bear!"

I can tell you one thing for sure, it was NOT a bear. I know a bear when I see one. I have seen black bear when I've been out walking. This thing did not look or act like a black bear. What I saw looked kind of like a human being and kind of like a gorilla mixed. It was only five or six feet in front of me.

It scared the tar out of me!

I've heard all kinds of stories about bigfoot and I never believed any of them. I heard something on TV about the Hillbilly Beast. I thought all that was made up until I saw this beast myself. I had seen pictures of what bigfoot was supposed to look like. What I saw kind of looked like that, but more human. It looked like a cross between a gorilla and a human.

When it saw me and stood up, I took off flying. I must have scared it, too. When I looked back, it was going up the mountain.

I kept thinking, "Good Lord! What was that?" I will never forget what it looked like.

I came home and told my brother, Ray, about it.

He said, "It sounds like you've seen a bigfoot. Maybe there's a nest of them around here or something. You never know."

I'm the one who saw it and I still have a hard time believing it. I always thought all that stuff was a bunch of monkey tales, you know, just a bunch of made up bull. Seeing it for myself changed my mind. I hope I never see it again!

The second one I saw happened about three years ago down below my house at a curve by Campbell's Branch. When it saw me, it went trotting up the mountain flat footed. The grade was straight up. It went up through there flying. It was monstrous looking.

I didn't want to go walking on the railroad track or down the road after that for a long time. I hope I never see whatever it was again.

My neighbor, Thomas Marcum, and his daddy have some footprints that came from a place they were hunting over by the Hensley Graveyard. The footprints are huge. They sure look like a bigfoot made them. It had two big toes and two little ones.

Thomas does bigfoot research. He says he's been doing it for about twenty years. He's talked to all kinds of people about what they've seen. Whatever this thing is, a lot of people are reporting seeing it in this area, or other creatures like it. I'm glad to know I'm not the only one who has seen it.

Thomas came to talk to me about it right after I saw the last one, then went back to the spot looking for any trace of it. I don't know if anyone will ever figure out exactly what it is.

I heard one person say they would like to catch one and keep it. Not me! I hope I never see one again!

Image by Brian Ingermann

Sasquatch Encounters
By Judith Victoria Hensley

If sasquatch existed on the continental United States territory when European settlers made their way across the vast new territory, it seemed to me that someone who could both read and write, perhaps a paid explorer, would have made written accounts of the creature, or at least recorded stories about the creature. When I began to look for such information on the internet, I was not disappointed.

In 1792 Jose Mariano Mozino took note of the Native American Indians and their fear of the creature we have come to call bigfoot. In his diary he wrote the following account.

"I do not know what to say about the matlox (sasquatch/ bigfoot), inhabitant of the mountainous districts of whom all have unbelievable fear. They imagine his body as very monstrous, all covered with stiff black bristle; a head similar to a human one but with much greater, sharper, and stronger fangs than those of the bar; extremely long arms; and toes and fingers armed with long curved claws. His shouts alone (they say) force those who hear them to the ground, and any unfortunate body he slaps is broken into a thousand pieces."

This account of Jose Mozino is recorded in the book, Sasquatch – *The Search for North America's Incredible Creature*, By Don Hunter and Rene Dahinden. The book was published by McClellans & Stweart, Inc. in 1973

In 1811, David Thompson, exploring the Canadian Rockies wrote in his diary, *"Continuing our journey in the afternoon, we came on the track of a large animal, the snow about six inches deep on the ice; I measured it. Four large toes of four inches in length to each a short claw; the ball of the foot sunk tree inches lower than the toes, the hinder part of the foot did not mark well. The length fourteen inches, by eight inches in breadth, walking from north to south, and having passed about six hours. We were in no humor to follow him. Its great size was not that of a bear."*

This account was also recorded in the book by Don Hunter and Rene Dahinden in 1973 as mentioned before.

Paul Kane *wrote in his journal in 1847, while exploring, "When we arrived at the mouth of the Kattlepoutal River, twenty-six miles from Vancouver (Washington), I stopped to make a sketch of the volcano, Mt. Saint Helens, from a distance I suppose to be about thirty or forty miles.*

This mountain has never been visited by either whites or Indians; the latter assert that it is inhabited by a race of beings of a different species, who are cannibals, and who they hold in great dread... these superstitions are taken from a man they say went into the mountains with another and escaped the fate of his companion who was eaten by the Skookums, or evil genii. I offered a considerable bribe to any Indian who would accompany me in its exploration but could not find one hardy enough to venture there."

This account was included in the book, *On the Track of the Sasquatch,* by John Green and published by Hancock House in 1980.

The Hagerstown Mail.

HAGERSTOWN, MD., FRIDAY, MAY 5, 1871.

THE TENNESSEE WILDMAN

The Jackson (Tenn.) *Whig* of the 13th instant says: "We learn that between Sobby and Crainsville, on what is called Piney, in McNairy county, a strange and frightful being has been observed for several weeks. He is said to be seven feet high, and possessed of great muscular power. His eyes are unusually large, and fiery red; his hair hangs in a tangled and matted mass of jet below his waist, and his beard reaches below his middle. His entire body is covered with hair, and his whole aspect is most frightful. He shuns the sight of men, but approaches with wild and horrid screams of delight every woman who is unaccompanied by a man. He sometimes, with great caution, approaches houses, and should he see a man he runs away with astonishing swiftness, leaping the tallest fences with the ease of a deer, defying alike the pursuit of men and dogs. He has frightened several women by attempting to carry them off, as well as by his horrid aspect, and the whole country around Sobby is in consternation. The citizens are now scouring the woods, and are determined either to capture of drive off the monster.

As I continued my research, some of the accounts were violent and bloody, not ending well for those who followed, pursued, hunted, or even accidentally came face to face with the creatures. They range on this continent from the French Canadian territories to the lower territories of what is now the continental United States.

In 1883, *The Daily Advocate, Newark Advocate* carried an article about "A Kentucky Wild Man" (which is my home state). I found it very interesting after having interviewed several eyewitnesses for this book project. Bigfoot sightings are nothing new in this state.

The article discovers the Kentucky Wild Man as being covered with thick hair, who refused to eat bread, but voraciously ate meat and liked fruit.

"Among the passengers the other night bound for New York from the west on the day express was a wild man who occupied a seat in smoking car No. 158. He was accompanied by James Harvey and Raymond Boyd, his captors, both of whom belong in Paducah County, Kentucky. They had three second-class tickets to New York, which privileges them to three seats in the smoking car of any first-class train. They were on their way to Bridgeport, Connectiut to make arrangements with P.T. Barnum to exhibit their prize in conjunction with the circus."

As much as I would love to see the mystery of sasquatch resolved in some logical manner, the 1883 article above establishes a fear in me of what would become of the creature if one of its species should ever be captured and contained. Such a specimen would certainly create a sensation with publicity for the captors, research for scientists, and curiosity seekers should such a creature be put on display. As much as I would like to see the many questions surrounding bigfoot sightings from around the world solved, I would not wish the creature to be hunted to extinction by those seeking fame and glory.

I've often though about what I would do personally if I were to capture a definitive photo proving the creature truly does exist. I might be thrilled and share it with a few friends, but ultimately, I would not want to create the sensation that would cause such a creature to become vulnerable to the technologies and scientific methods of modern man.

Sightings continue around the world with reports coming in on a regular basis.

For those interested in pursuing their own studies and research, www.bigfootencounters.com lists over 4,000 articles or newspaper reports about this creature.

In searching for information, it is important to look for accounts under the term "wild man," as well as "bigfoot," and sasquatch. Accounts such as these are numerous. The term "bigfoot" did not occur until the mid1950s when a newspaper, *The Province,* ran an article with a picture of a huge plaster cast of a footprint. That article referred to the creature which made it as "bigfoot" and the term stuck. This remains the most popular common name used today in reference of the creature.

Go.newspapers.com lists 187,585 articles matching the search for "bigfoot" and 307,780 that match the search of "Wildman."

My purpose for compiling these stories is simple. I am a story gatherer. It is not my goal to argue for the existence of bigfoot or against. I simply wanted to create a venue for people to share their stories and get them in print to become part of the folklore of this region and also to become part of a broader network of individuals who express similar encounters.

I am persuaded that for every single story that is formally recorded orally or in print, there are a dozen more which are never shared because people fear the ridicule that might follow. If people were confident that they would be listened to, their stories valued, and their encounters legitimized, I am convinced there would be many more on record.

This book is my attempt to help make that happen.

WELCOME
WV

The Woodbooger Grill
By Judith Victoria Hensley

Bigfoot is known by many names. In Norton, Virginia he is known by the name of Woodbooger. The town has created a culture around the theme of the Woodbooger. A drive through Norton shows evidence that the local people support this concept. There is even a Woodbooger Festival each summer.

I recently made a visit to the Woodbooger Grill in Norton, Virginia. The food was great, and the theme was fun. I think the burger was one of the best I've ever eaten anywhere.

When I asked for permission to snap some photos in the restaurant, I was granted permission to do so by the owner.

Especially interesting to me was the challenge for patrons to draw pictures of the woodbooger on a napkin while they waited on their orders. Once completed, they are hung on a designated bulletin board for others to enjoy.

The city has designated a portion of the Flag Rock Recreation Area as the "Woodbooger Sanctuary." A large statue of the creature can be found there.

Local merchants sell a wide variety of merchandise, featuring the Woodbooger. Although no one could tell me if the whole thing was started by a local encounter with bigfoot, the town has certainly popularized this theme.

With permission from their management, I am sharing some of the napkin drawings created by patrons to hang on the public bulletin board.

Anonymous Napkin Artist from the Woodbooger Grill in Norton, Virginia

Look a human!
Run!

If you have a story about your own eyewitness encounter of bigfoot, or a story you know from a reliable source (such as family stories handed down), that you would like to contribute to an upcoming book, please follow the guideline below. You must fill out and sign the form on the following page and submit it with your digital signature or via snail mail before your story will be considered. Original artwork will also be considered.

Please answer these questions.

1. Tell a little about yourself (short), such as job, time spent in the woods, etc.
2. When did the encounter take place?
   - Time of Day
   - Season of the year or month
3. Where did the event take place (as specifically as possible)?
4. Were you with anyone else at the time and did they also see the creature?
5. What were you doing at the time of the bigfoot sighting/encounter?
6. Describe what you saw, especially how the creature looked or behaved.
7. Describe your reaction to the event and the reaction of other people if appropriate.

THERE IS NO PAYMENT FOR STORIES ACCEPTED. IT IS STRICTLY ON A VOLUNTARY BASIS FROM PEOPLE WHO WOULD LIKE TO SEE THEIR STORY IN PRINT, and share them with other interested readers/researchers.

Completed projects will be available on Amazon.com and Kindle

I, _______________________________________, am submitting my
story and/or artwork for consideration in a future
book project about Bigfoot or other cryptids. I will be
notified when such a project is completed if my story
and/or artwork is included.

I understand that there will be **no purchase of my
story individually or my original artwork**, and **NO
CASH PAYMENT for my story/artwork** and that I am
submitting it strictly on a voluntary basis because I
want to share the story/artwork in print with full credit
given to me for my story and/or artwork.

There may be editing purposes for grammar,
punctuation, and space within the book set-up, but the
actual story will not be altered in any other way. I trust
the integrity of the story teller to be truthful and share
ONLY non-fiction accounts.

____

Signature   Date

____

Printed name as you wish it to appear in the book

____

Address

____

____

Submit digitally to: **judith99@bellsouth.net**
Submit by post office mail to: **Judith V. Hensley   P.O.
Box 982   Loyall, KY   40854**

www.ingramcontent.com/pod-product-compliance
Lightning Source LLC
Chambersburg PA
CBHW051746250726
48659CB00001B/269